television

tire

tiger

toe

t

tunnel

train

truck

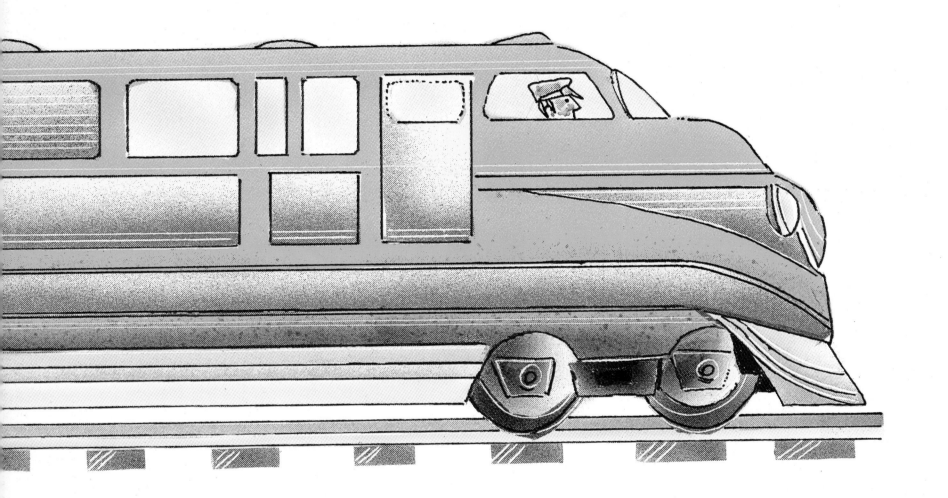

This is a train.

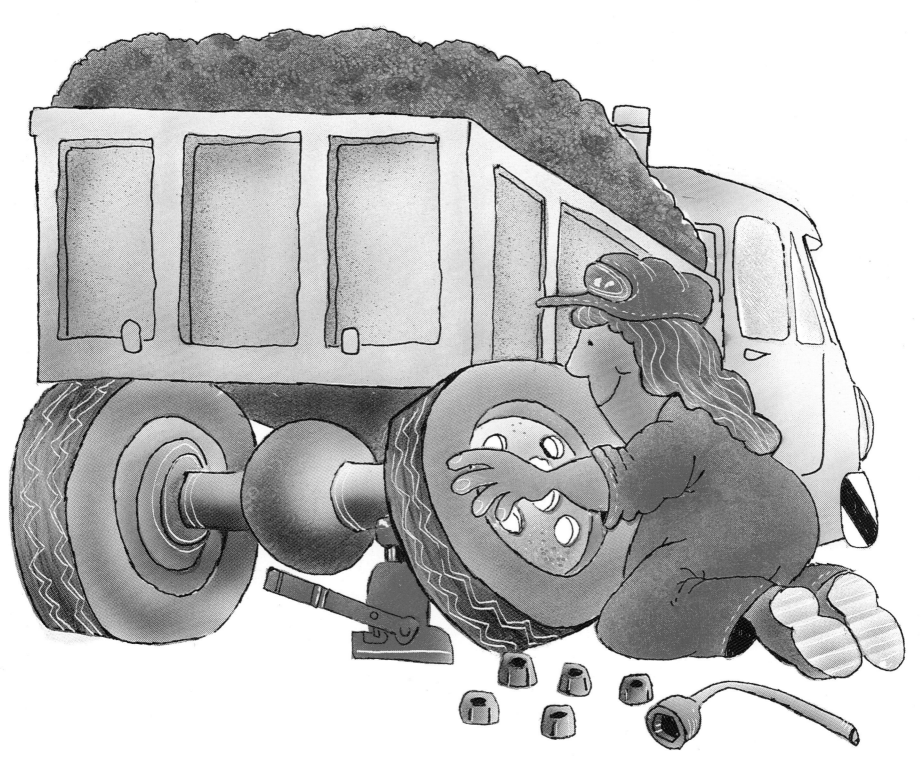

This is a tire
on a truck.

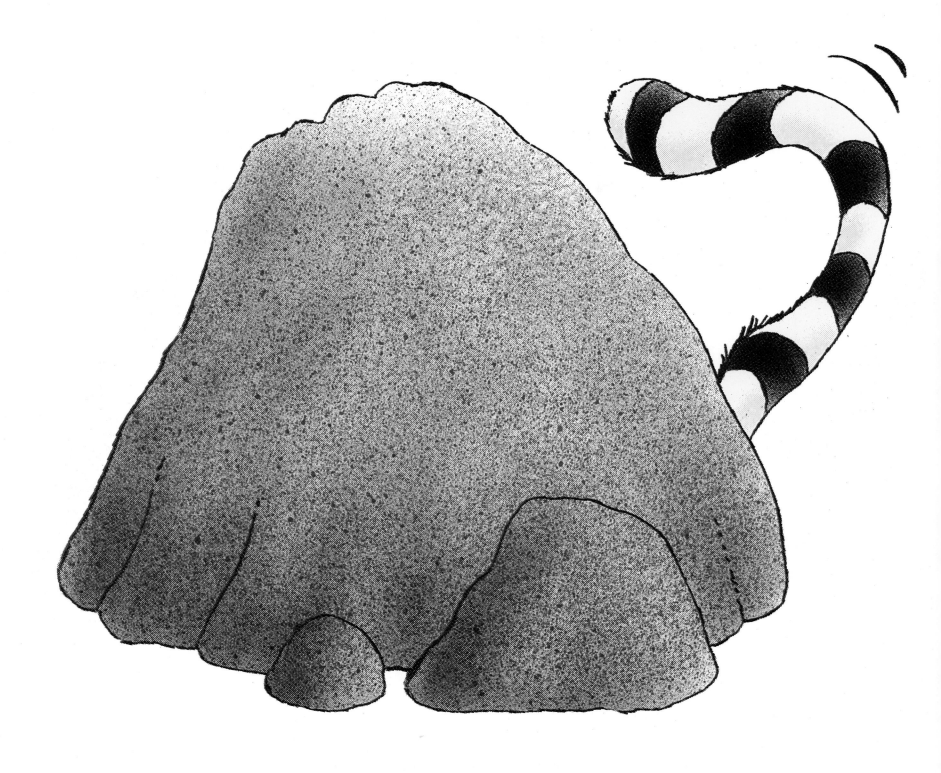

This is a **t**ail.

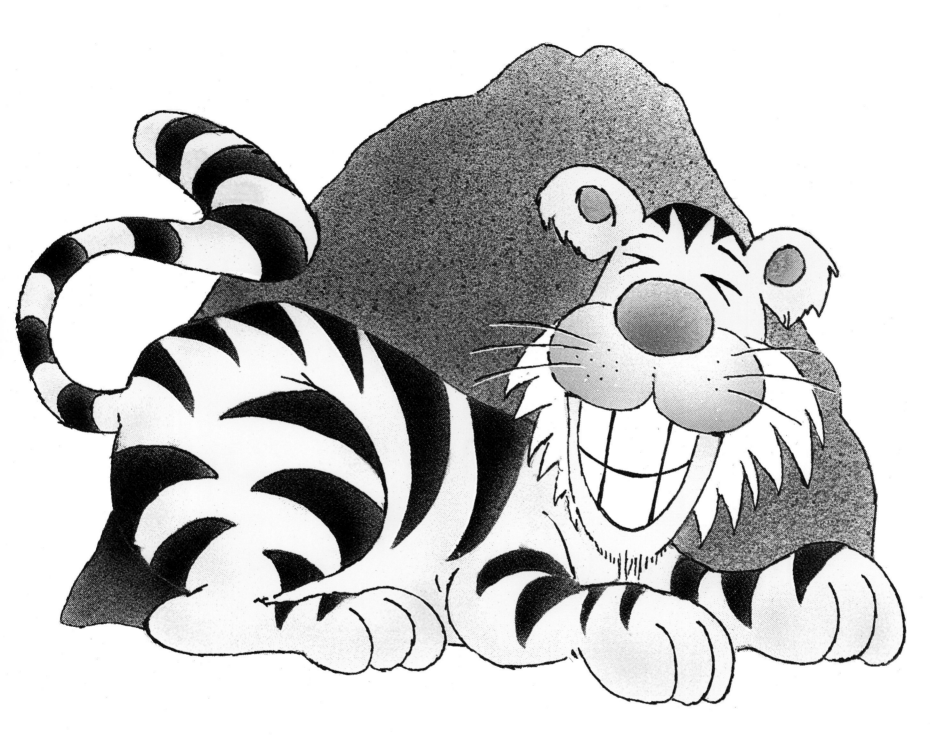

This is a **t**ail
on a **t**iger!

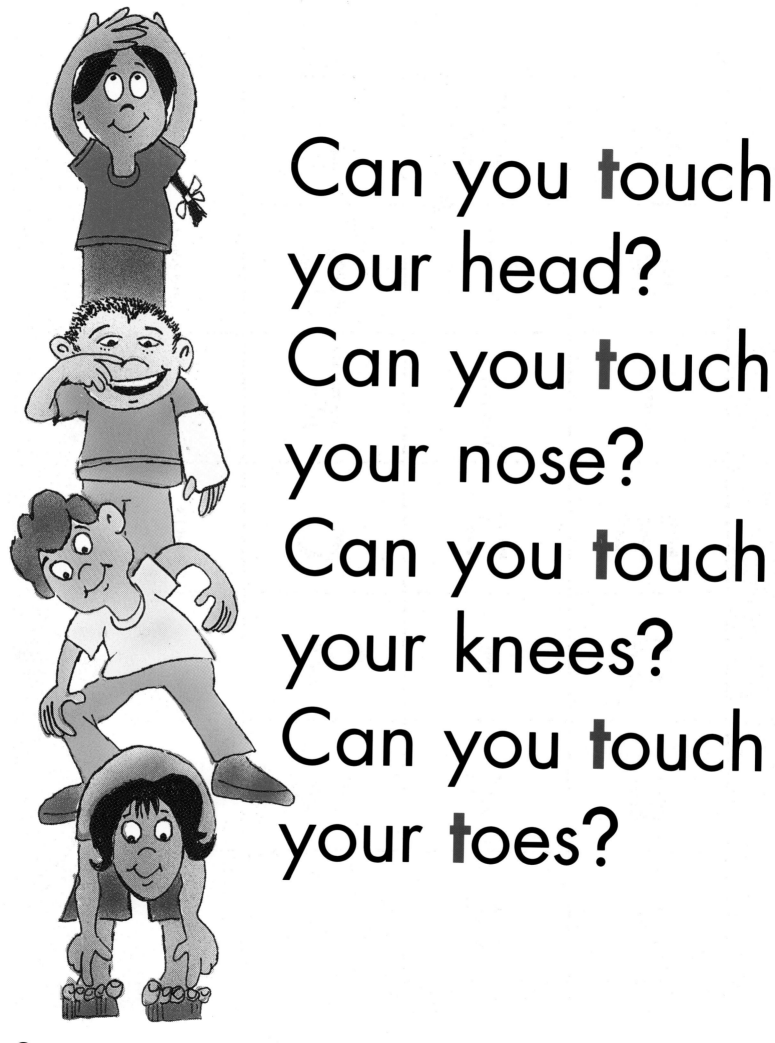

Can you touch your head?
Can you touch your nose?
Can you touch your knees?
Can you touch your toes?